Quick Tricks
for Language

by Barbara F. Backer
illustrated by Marilynn G. Barr

Dedication:

To Don who knows the unspoken language.

Publisher: Roberta Suid
Design & Production: Standing Watch Productions
Cover Design: David Hale

CONTENTS

INTRODUCTION

When children are born, their spoken vocabulary of words is zero. Their expressive language consists of crying. Next they begin cooing. A few months later they babble, stringing together repetitive sounds like ba-ba-ba-ba and ma-ma-ma-ma. Somewhere near the end of their first year they begin speaking single, recognizable words.

Before the end of their second year, children are forming sentences. Between ages two and four, they learn to use some of the basic structure of their native language. As their small muscles strengthen and become more refined, children are able to properly pronounce more and more sounds and are able to add more words to their spoken vocabularies.

Children accumulate a speaking vocabulary of about 2,500 words by the time they are six. Between ages three and six, their vocabulary more than triples. Their "receptive vocabulary," words they understand when they hear them but that they are not yet speaking, is even larger. Adults help them by surrounding children with a rich language environment. Reading to children, singing with them, saying simple rhymes together, explaining to them what they are doing and what will happen next—all of these enrich children's vocabularies. But language is not just about listening and speaking. It also includes reading and writing. Before age six, many children are interested in forming letters and experimenting with writing. They begin recognizing familiar words in the environment and written letters that they see regularly. These are the beginning stages of writing and reading, and they develop together.

This book contains activities that help children develop language skills. These "Quick Tricks" are designed around children's interests. Preschool children learn best from hands-on experiences with learning materials. Therefore, your children will be encouraged to talk and be excited about the learning, and they will manipulate items to learn more about their language qualities. The activities are meant to be enjoyed in a casual, informal setting and atmosphere. The emphasis is on having a language experience, not in getting a right or wrong answer. If your children offer incorrect information, ask them how they figured that out. Remember that young children's brains have not finished developing. Through repetition of activities like those in this book, they build their knowledge and their problem-solving abilities.

While you can use the activities in any order, they are arranged with early chapters building skills needed for concepts in the later chapters. For example, children with poor listening skills can't learn vocabulary from hearing spoken words.

Most chapters include a letter for parents. The letters inform parents of what their children are learning in school and offer a Quick Trick for continuing the learning at home. To keep the language simple, chapters alternate between referring to children as "he" or "she."

EXPRESSIVE LANGUAGE: CHANTING TRICKS

Every language has its own distinct rhythm. Chanting helps children become aware of the rhythm of language and over time can help them learn to regulate the rhythm of their own speech.

Chanting is natural for children. Listen to them as they play. They'll sing out, "I've got the red car," or they'll taunt each other, "You can't come to my birthday."

To enhance children's awareness of the rhythm of chanting, sway back and forth to the chant's rhythm, or have children tap rhythmically on their bodies as they chant. For interaction, let everyone find a partner. While chanting, one of the pair uses a hand to make a back-and-forth "windshield wiper" action on the partner's back. For another, have one of the pair sit behind the other and tap the partner on alternating shoulders in rhythm with the chant. Switch partners and repeat.

Birthday Chants
A Quick Trick with the "Happy Birthday" Song

Gather These Materials:
none

Where: at a birthday celebration

How: Use the rhythm of the "Happy Birthday" song to create chants that relate to birthdays. When the birthday honoree receives a present, he can chant, "Oh, I thank you very much." When guests arrive at a birthday party, all who are already gathered chant, "We're so happy you're here."

Variation:
Create chants for the rhythms of other popular songs.

This activity also helps children learn about:
receiving gifts and guests graciously.

Chanting in Our World
A Quick Trick with Things You See Around You

Gather These Materials:
none

Where: anywhere

How: When you and the children are outside, chant in monotone about something you see:

I see a <u>bug</u>,
I see a <u>bug</u>,
I see a <u>bug</u>,
I see a <u>bug</u>.

Point out the bug to your children or let them look for it and point it out.

Substitute other things you see for the underlined word.

Variations:
Let your children take turns chanting about something they see while you and the remaining children look for the item.
With older preschool children, have each person in turn chant about something larger than the previously mentioned item.

This activity also helps children learn about:
the variety of things in their environment.

Quick Tricks for Language ©2001 Monday Morning Books, Inc.

Drinking Milk
A Quick Trick with a Cup of Milk

Gather These Materials:
a cup of milk for each child (optional)

Where: anywhere

How: Serve each child a cup of milk (or give each a "pretend" cup of milk). Before they drink their milk, let them enjoy this chant:

> A-B-CDE
> A cup of milk is good for me.
> F-G-HIJ
> I like to drink it every day.
> K-L-MNO
> I like it cold, and that is so.
> P-Q-RST
> Milk is white as you can see.
> U-V-WXY
> Milk is good, oh me, oh my.
> Z-Z-ZZZ
> A cup of milk is good for me.

Variation:
Make up chants about other foods using the format of the chant above.

> A-B-CDE
> Eating carrots is good for me.
> F-G-HIJ
> I like to eat them every day.
> K-L-MNO
> Carrots are sweet, and that is so.
> P-Q-RST
> Carrots are orange as you can see.
> U-V-WXY
> Carrots are good, oh me, oh my.
> Z-Z-ZZZ
> Eating carrots is good for me.

This activity also helps children learn about:
the alphabet.

Everyday Chants
A Quick Trick with Familiar Rhythmic Phrases

Gather These Materials:
none

Where: anywhere

How: Listen for an everyday phrase that can be turned into a chant. "Cash or credit?" is a good example. With the children, chant the words several times exaggerating the syllables that are emphasized. Now, have children use their hands to clap out the rhythm while they chant the words. Finally, have them clap out the rhythm while they are silent.

Repeat the activity with other rhythmic phrases like these: "Paper or plastic?" "Believe it or not."

Variations:
Chant a child's name several times, then proceed as above. Continue until each child's name has been used.

This activity also helps children learn about:
matching and nonmatching rhythms.

Quick Tricks for Language ©2001 Monday Morning Books, Inc.

Excellent Egg Salad
A Quick Trick with Hard-Cooked Eggs

Gather These Materials:
waxed paper
cooled, hard-cooked eggs, 1 for each child
small plastic bowls, 1 for each child
plastic knives with serrated blades, 1 for each child
celery, a few ribs
spoons, 1 for each child
mayonnaise
forks, 1 for each child
salt and pepper or seasoned salt (optional)
bread, 2 slices for each child

Where: at a table in the kitchen

How: Place a large piece of waxed paper on the table in front of each child. This will serve as a place mat and a cutting board. Let each child peel one egg and place it in his own plastic bowl. Show the children how to use the knife to chop the egg in the bowl. Demonstrate how to put the celery on the waxed paper and use the knife to slice or chop the celery. Have children add their celery to their chopped eggs.

Help each child measure out the amount of mayonnaise he needs (just enough to hold the mixture together) and seasoning to taste. Place the mixtures in the refrigerator to chill. When the egg salad is ready, have children spread it on bread for sandwiches.

While you are making the salad, or waiting for it to chill, say the following chant/rap together. Emphasize the underlined words.

> Cook the <u>eggs</u> in a <u>pot</u>; <u>cook</u>, cook, <u>cook</u>.
> Peel the <u>eggs</u> when they're <u>cool</u>; <u>peel</u>, peel, <u>peel</u>.
> Chop the <u>eggs</u> in the <u>bowl</u>; <u>chop</u>, chop, <u>chop</u>.
> Shake in <u>pepper</u> and some <u>salt</u>; <u>shake</u>, shake, <u>shake</u>.
> Stir some <u>mayon</u>naise in the <u>bowl</u>; <u>stir</u>, stir, <u>stir</u>.
> Spread it <u>on some</u> yummy <u>bread</u>; <u>spread</u>, spread
>   <u>spread</u>.
> Eat it <u>up</u>, eat it <u>up</u>; <u>yum</u>, yum, <u>yum</u>.
> Eat it <u>up</u>, eat it <u>up</u>; <u>yum</u>, yum, <u>yum</u>.

This activity also helps children learn about:
names of ingredients.

EXPRESSIVE LANGUAGE: SINGING TRICKS

Most children sing naturally, singing to themselves while they play. While they are singing songs they've learned from others or songs they make up themselves, children are learning about the rhythm of language. Singing children learn about rhyming, too, because many songs have rhyming words at the end of each phrase.

Sing along with tapes or disks recorded especially for children, but also let children hear a variety of music, both instrumental and vocal. Each type of music (classical, rock, music from other countries, pop, blues, swing) has its own rhythm. Hearing these differences helps children become more aware of other rhythms, including the rhythm of speech.

Silly Songs
A Quick Trick with Familiar Songs

Gather These Materials:
tape or CD of children's songs (optional)
tape or CD player (optional)

Where: anywhere

How: Sing a number of children's songs with your children until they are familiar with the words. If you don't know any appropriate songs, listen with your children to recordings made for them. Now change the words of the songs to fit experiences in your life.

Example:
Tune: "Row, Row, Row Your Boat"

Carry, carry, carry the blocks
Gently to the shelves.
Merrily, merrily, merrily, merrily
Life is but a dream.

Don't worry that the last line doesn't rhyme.

Variation:
Use a tape recorder to record the children and yourself as you sing made-up songs and other songs. Play the recorded tape and sing along with yourselves.

This activity also helps children learn about:
rhythm.

Singing Jingles
A Quick Trick with Advertising Jingles

Gather These Materials:
none

Where: anywhere

How: Take advantage of children's interest in radio and TV jingles. When your children begin singing the jingles they've heard, sing along with them. "Request" that they sing specific jingles.

Variation:
Make up new words or silly words to the jingles and sing them together.

This activity also helps children learn about:
listening.

Tickling
A Quick Trick with a Soft Cloth

Gather These Materials:
a soft cloth for each child

Where: anywhere

How: Give each child a soft cloth to use as a tickling prop. Sing the song below, tickling the mentioned body part with the soft cloth. Substitute a different body part's name for the underlined word each time you sing the song. Let the children take turns suggesting a body part to tickle.

Tune: "Happy Birthday"

I tickle my <u>toes</u>.
I tickle my <u>toes</u>.
I tickle and I giggle;
I tickle my <u>toes</u>.

Variation:
Children can tickle with their fingers instead of using cloths.

This activity also helps children learn about:
names of body parts.

Quick Tricks for Language ©2001 Monday Morning Books, Inc.

Stop and Listen
A Quick Trick with Movement

Gather These Materials:
none

Where: anywhere there is space for vigorous movement

How: Encourage your children to move as suggested in the song below. At the words "Stop and listen," they stop all movement and noise so they can hear the suggested movement in the next verse. As soon as they hear how to move, they move again, singing the new words as they go.

Tune: "London Bridge"

We are <u>marching</u> all around,
All around, all around.
We are <u>marching</u> all around,
STOP and listen.

We are <u>jumping</u> all around
All around, all around.
We are <u>jumping</u> all around,
STOP and listen.

Variation:
Substitute other motions for those underlined in the song. Suggestions: walking, hopping, skipping, crawling, rolling, tip-toeing, scooting.

This activity also helps children learn about:
names of different ways to move.

EXPRESSIVE LANGUAGE: PUPPET TRICKS

> Puppets offer children an outlet for the spoken word. It's fun to take on another identity and say outrageous things. Animal puppets can talk to humans and to each other. All of these give your children the freedom and opportunity to take on new roles and use new words. Even shy children will often speak through a puppet.
>
> Make many puppets with your children. Encourage them to let the puppets perform. Puppets like to sing and dance and recite simple rhymes, and children like to make up silly things for puppets to say and sing. Children and puppets are a natural combination.

Hand Puppets
A Quick Trick with Children's Hands

Gather These Materials:
washable markers

Where: anywhere

How: Have your children make hand puppets by using washable markers to draw a face on each of their hands. The children's fingers are their puppets' hair. When the children complete the creations, let the "puppets" put on a show, singing any of the children's favorite songs.

Wash hands thoroughly when through; otherwise, children's perspiring hands will leave colored smudges on everything they touch.

Variation:
Some creative children may draw a "profile" view, using the thumb as a large nose.

This activity also helps children learn about:
creative thinking.

Envelope Puppet
A Quick Trick with a Used Envelope

Gather These Materials:
used envelope for each child
construction paper scraps
scissors
glue or glue sticks
markers

Where: at a table

How: When you open your mail, slit the narrow end of the envelope, not the top of the flap. Remove mail and save the envelopes for this puppet-making activity. Have each child put an envelope face-down on the table with the slit at the bottom. Have the children use the remaining materials to make eyes, mouth, ears, and other features, decorating the envelopes to look like people or animals. Help the children slip their hands into the decorated envelopes, and encourage them to create spontaneous puppet shows of conversation between their puppets.

Variation:
Some children will add hair, arms, legs, and clothing. Encourage them to tell you what they have done and how they have done it.

This activity also helps children learn about:
names of facial features and body parts.

Clothespin Puppet
A Quick Trick with a Wooden Clothespin

Gather These Materials:
fine-tip felt markers, any colors
one-piece, solid wooden clothespins (without springs)
fabric scraps
small stapler

Where: at a table

How: Have the children use the felt markers to draw facial features on clothespins. Let each child wrap his clothespin in a fabric scrap for clothing and staple the scrap so it will stay on. If desired, the children can use markers to add shoes or other items.
   Encourage your children to make several characters so they can act out spontaneous scenes and have their puppets talk to each other.

Variation:
Children can use glue and construction paper scraps for puppet clothing.

This activity also helps children learn about:
unusual uses for ordinary items.

Quick Tricks for Language ©2001 Monday Morning Books, Inc.

A Baggy Cat
A Quick Trick with a Paper Bag

Gather These Materials:
lunch-size paper bags, 1 for each child
a 4-inch (10-cm) triangle cut from construction paper, 1 for each child
two 1-inch (2.5-cm) triangles cut from construction paper, 1 set for each child
glue or glue sticks
construction paper scraps
markers

Where: at a table

How: Give each child a lunch-size paper bag and the triangles. Have the children put the paper bags on the table in front of themselves with the "flap" (bottom) on top and the opening close to the table's edge. Have them glue the large triangle, point down, onto the bag's "flap" for a cat's head. Place the bottom point of the large triangle just above the flap's bottom edge.

Have the children glue the smaller triangles onto the top of the large triangle for the cat's ears. Encourage them to use construction paper scraps and markers to add other features—eyes, nose, whiskers, paws—to the cat's face and body.

When the glue is dry, have children put their hands inside their cat puppets and move the puppets around while they sing the following song:

Tune: "The Farmer in the Dell"

I am a baggy cat,
A saggy, baggy cat.
I jumped into my owner's lap,
To take a little nap.

I purred in my sleep.
A noise so low and deep.
My owner jumped up to his feet
And stopped my little sleep.

I woke up from my nap.
My owner lost his lap.
I tumbled onto the floor,
Then I ran out the door.

I am a baggy cat.
A saggy, baggy cat.
I'd like to take another nap
But my owner lost his lap.

Variation:
Make materials available for the children to create other paper bag puppets.

This activity also helps children learn about:
rhyming.

Dear Parents,

In school we have been learning about the rhythm of language while we say different chants, sing songs, and play with puppets. Chanting, singing, and a love of rhythm are natural for children. You can build on your child's awareness of rhythm by swaying together to music while you sing or when you listen to music. Together you can make up simple songs and chants of your own. Cheer together for a sports team: "Go, Tigers, go! Go, Tigers, go!" Chant as you "march" together to the bathroom: "Time for a bath. Time for a bath." Sing together to recordings or tunes or advertising jingles you hear on the radio.

Encourage your child to play with the puppets he makes at school. Provide him with paper, scissors, and glue, and encourage him to make additional puppets at home. He can help the puppets sing songs, chant rhythms, and perform advertising jingles.

The "Quick Trick" below offers another idea for chanting and moving in rhythm. Why not give it a try?

A Quick Trick with My Body

Gather These Materials:
none

Where: anywhere

How: Using a slow, steady beat and chanting in a monotone, re-peatedly touch, pat, or gently tap one body part and chant about your actions:

> I touch my <u>head</u>.
> I touch my <u>head</u>.

Repeat the phrase eight times, then select another body part to touch or tap and begin again.

LISTENING SKILLS: LISTENING TRICKS

Children learn about language by listening to it. They absorb new vocabulary by hearing words used again and again. After they learn to recognize letters, they begin to understand that words that start the same way, *bear*, *ball*, *bath*, and *beach*, all begin with the same letter, b. This is the start of learning to "sound out" words.

Give your children opportunities to listen to the radio, recorded stories, music, storytellers, and conversation. Read picture books with them and read poetry to them. Have a storytelling time when no books are used. When there are no pictures to look at, children must depend completely on their listening skills to understand the story.

Listen to your children when they talk to you. When possible, stop what you are doing and make eye contact while you listen. Model what you want your children to learn.

Who Do I Hear?
A Quick Trick with a Tape Recorder

Gather These Materials:
tape recorder
recording tape

Where: anywhere

How: Use the tape recorder to record the sounds of your children playing, especially when they are talking to each other or to themselves. Don't let them know you are recording. Later, play back the tape. Children love to listen to themselves and others and to relive the conversations. Can they identify the voices?

Variation:
Record stories as you read to your children. Show them how they can later listen to the taped stories while they hold the book and follow along.

This activity also helps children learn about:
prereading skills when they read while following along with recorded books.

If I had a lamb I would take it to school too!

Fly Away Birds
A Quick Trick with Bird Stickers

Gather These Materials:
five commercially available stickers with bird pictures on them
five 2-inch (5-cm) squares cut from index cards

Where: at a table or on the floor

How: Place a sticker on each index card square. Place the five cards in a row where your children can see them. Count the birds together. Say the following rhyme and have children, in place, act out the kitty-cat's actions. Have a child remove a card each time a bird "flies away."

Five little birds sat in a tree today.
Along came kitty-cat, and one flew away.
Four little birds sat in a tree today.
The kitty-cat mee-owed, and one flew away.
Three little birds sat in a tree today.
The kitty-cat stretched, and one flew away.
Two little birds sat in a tree today.
The kitty-cat scampered, and one flew away.
One little bird sat in a tree today.
The kitty-cat ran up the tree, and one flew away.
No little birds are in the tree right now.
Kitty-cat is in the tree,
Saying "mee-ow, mee-ow, mee-ow."

Variation:
Place a bird sticker on each of the fingers and the thumb of one hand. Hold up your hand while saying the rhyme, and "hide" one finger each time a bird "flies away". Let the other hand be the kitty-cat.

This activity also helps children learn about:
counting.

Quick Tricks for Language ©2001 Monday Morning Books, Inc.

Following Directions
A Quick Trick with Everyday Items

Gather These Materials:
everyday items such as a red mitten, puppet, blue circle, yellow
paper, red napkin, paper clip

Where: at a table or on the floor

How: With a small group of children (or with one child), spread three
items in front of you. Have the children, in turn, follow your directions.
In turn, give the children easy, one-step directions like these: "Put
your finger on something red." "Put your finger beside the puppet."
"Hide your finger under the circle." "Be sure that your directions are
specific to the items in front of you."

As your children's skill improves, add another step to the directions with instructions like these: "Put this paper clip between something red and something yellow." "Put a puppet on a circle." "Put a
paper clip on the puppet and put a red napkin on top of that."

Variation:
Add more items to the display as children's skill increases.

This activity also helps children learn about:
names of items, shape names, and color words.

Hide your finger under the circle.

Reading Together
A Quick Trick with Storybooks

Gather These Materials:
a storybook with pictures on each page

Where: anywhere that your children can see the book
while you read it

How: Read to your children every day. Talk about the story. Ask questions like these: What did the main character want? What happened? Where did the story take place? Do you like the book? Why or why not?

It isn't necessary to discuss every book every time you read. The important thing is to read regularly.

Variation:
Let your children ask you questions about the story.

This activity also helps children learn about:
focusing on the story that is being read.

Quick Tricks for Language ©2001 Monday Morning Books, Inc.

Rhythm Box
A Quick Trick with an Empty Box and a Spoon

Gather These Materials:
empty cardboard boxes, any size, 1 for each child plus an
extra for yourself
cooking spoons, any kind, 1 for each child plus an extra for yourself

Where: anywhere

How: Give each of your children an empty box and a large cooking
spoon. Keep a box and spoon for yourself. Tap out a simple rhythm
of three to six beats on your box. Ask your children to copy the
rhythm and play it back to you. Repeat each rhythm/play-back
cycle several times to offer children many opportunities to hear the
rhythm and duplicate it. Alert the children each time you are going
to change the rhythm. Here are some suggested rhythms to
get you started:

    1, 2, 3, stop; 1, 2, 3, stop; 1, 2, 3, stop
    1, 2, 3, 4, stop; 1, 2, 3, 4, stop; 1, 2, 3, 4, stop
    1, 2, 3, stop, stop; 1, 2, 3, stop, stop; 1, 2, 3, stop, stop
    1, 2, 3, stop, stop, stop; 1, 2, 3, stop, stop, stop; 1, 2, 3, stop, stop, stop
    1, 2-3; 1, 2-3; 1, 2-3
    1, 2-3, 4, stop; 1, 2-3, 4, stop; 1, 2-3, 4, stop

    Note: Each "stop" counts as a whole beat of rhythm with no
tapping on the box.

Variation:
After your children have practiced this activity, let them take
turns tapping out a rhythm for others to copy.

This activity also helps children learn about:
listening carefully.

What Do I See?
A Quick Trick with Common Items

Gather These Materials:
assorted common items (see below)

Where: anywhere

How: Place a few different items in front of you. Tell the children you will describe one of the items and they should take turns guessing which you are describing. When you first play the game, choose items that are distinctly different (apple, fork, napkin, sweater). Pause after each clue to give the children time to process the information. Give clues like these:

It keeps you warm. It has sleeves. (The sweater.)
It is sharp at one end. You use it to eat. (The fork.)
You can eat it. (The apple.)

As your children become more skilled at listening, use items that have similarities (red apple, red paper, yellow banana, yellow truck), and give clues like these:

It is red. It is a fruit. You can eat it. It is juicy. (Red apple.)
It is red. You can cut it and glue it. You can write on it. (Red paper.)

Variation:
Look around you and describe an object or person that you and all of the children can see. Have your children listen to the simple description and, in turn, guess what or whom you've described.

This activity also helps children learn about:
descriptive vocabulary.

Quick Tricks for Language ©2001 Monday Morning Books, Inc.

Which One?
A Quick Trick with Paper Shapes

Gather These Materials:
precut paper shapes (available at school supply stores, or cut your own)

Where: on the floor or at a table

How: Place five or six different shapes on the floor—for example, a snowflake, pumpkin, frog, umbrella, and rabbit. Have your children look at the shapes and name them. Now ask them simple questions about items represented by the shapes, and have them answer by naming the correct shape. Keep the questions simple. The object of this activity is to focus on listening skills, not to trick the players.

"What is cold and falls from the sky?" (snowflake)
"What can we turn into a jack-o'-lantern?" (pumpkin)
"What keeps us dry when it is raining?" (umbrella)
"What is an animal that hops?" (rabbit or frog—both are correct)
"What hops and has long ears?" (rabbit)
"What hops and lives in a pond?" (frog)
"What is white?" (rabbit or snowflake)
"Which of these is green?" (frog or umbrella)

Repeat the activity with other shapes.

Variation:
Use stickers instead of precut shapes.

This activity also helps children learn about:
listening for details.

LISTENING SKILLS: RHYMING TRICKS

To understand rhyming, children must be able to hear that the rhyming words sound the same <u>at the end of the word</u>. Don't try to "teach" rhyming. It is a skill that usually emerges between ages four and five in children who have a lot of experience with language.

Airplane Action
A Quick Trick with Craft Sticks

Gather These Materials:
2 craft sticks for each child
white glue
markers

Where: at a table to make the airplanes
anywhere to fly the airplane

How: Have your children make small airplanes by gluing two craft sticks together so that one stick is the airplane's fuselage and the other forms the wings. When the glue has dried, have the children use markers to decorate the planes. Together, sing this song while the children hold and "fly" the planes. Encourage them to bend, stretch, and reach as they act out the song.

Tune: "Happy Birthday"

My airplane flies low,
My airplane flies high,
It flies over houses,
Way up in the sky.

My airplane flies low,
My airplane flies high,
And when it is finished,
It comes down from the sky.

It flies over cities,
It flies over trees.
It flies over Mommy,
And it flies over me.

Variation:
Let your children suggest other places the airplane flies and substitute these in the song.

This activity also helps children learn about:
words indicating position: low, high, over.

Hello, Mother Goose
A Quick Trick with Mother Goose Rhymes

Gather These Materials:
books of Mother Goose rhymes

Where: anywhere

How: With your children, read rhymes from various collections of
Mother Goose rhymes. Repeat favorites again and again. Say the
rhymes together in high, squeaky voices and in low, deep voices.
Say them very slowly or very quickly.

Variation:
Repeat a familiar Mother Goose rhyme but omit the word at the end
of each line. Encourage your children to say the omitted word. Over
time, omit more and more words until the children are saying the
entire rhyme.

This activity also helps children learn about:
memorizing short rhymes.

It Sounds Like....
A Quick Trick with Paper Shapes

Gather These Materials:
commercially available, precut paper shapes

Where: at a table or on the floor

How: Place assorted precut shapes (pig, flower, snowflake, turkey, and so on) on the table or floor. Children listen to you as you say, "Point to the one that sounds like <u>wig</u>." In turn, children point to a shape that has a sound that rhymes with the word you said.

For each turn, substitute another word for the underlined word until you have provided many rhymes for each shape and every child has had a turn.

Sample things for you to say:
"Point to the one that sounds like <u>shower</u>." (flower)
"Point to the one that sounds like <u>no cake</u>." (snowflake)
"Point to the one that sounds like <u>jerky</u>." (turkey)

In later turns, use other sounds for these same shapes. For example, *dig, big, jig,* and *fig* all rhyme with *pig. Hour, sour,* and *power* rhyme with *flower.* Use nonsense words, too, like *kig, vig, zower, vower,* and *jower.*

Variation:
If a child points to the correct shape, let her take the shape and keep it. Have her add another shape to the group on the table or floor before the next child has a turn.

This activity also helps children learn about:
paying attention.

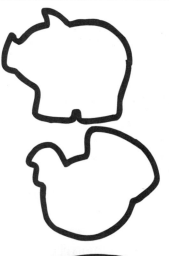

Shower sounds like flower.

Silly Rhymes
A Quick Trick with Imagination

Gather These Materials:
none

Where: anywhere

How: With your children, make up silly rhymes. Here are a few examples to get your started:

> Sue has two eyes on her face.
> She can take them anyplace.
>
> I'd like to ride a horse that's brown.
> I'd ride him fast, you see.
> Up the hills and then back down.
> Watch out for that elm tree!

Variation:
Make up the first line and most of the second line of a rhyme. Challenge children to add the last word of the second line. Younger children who don't yet understand the concept of rhyming may supply a word that doesn't sound like the last word of the first line. Don't worry about this; the skill will come in time. Accept the silly answers, and giggle with the children.

This activity also helps children learn about:
the rhythm and richness of language.

Soupy Rhyme
A Quick Trick with Soup Bowls

Gather These Materials:
5 soup bowls

Where: at a table

How: Place five soup bowls in a row on the table. Say the rhyme below and have a child remove one bowl at the end of each stanza. Substitute the names of children in the group or of others they suggest for the underlined names. Using the word *zero* in the last stanza helps children learn that it is a number that means none.

Five bowls of soup were sitting on the table.
<u>Dad</u> ate one bowl as well as he was able.

Four bowls of soup were sitting on the table.
<u>Mom</u> ate one bowl as well as she was able.

(Continue until no bowls are left)

Zero bowls of soup are sitting on the table.
Bring more bowls as soon as you are able.

Variation:
Count the remaining soup bowls before each stanza.

This activity also helps children learn about:
number names.

Wiggly Fish
A Quick Trick with Paper and Newspaper

Gather These Materials:
pencil
paper
scissors
markers
stapler and staples
newspaper
hole punch
yarn or heavy string

Where: at a table

How: Help the children cut two large identical fish shapes (12 inches/30 cm from head to tail). Help each child staple her two fish together along the edges, leaving a wide space open at the top. Have the children decorate their fish on both sides with markers. Hold each fish while its creator lightly stuffs it with crumpled newspaper. Staple the opening closed.

Punch a hole at the top of the fish and attach string or yarn. Have the children hold the ends of their yarn and "swim" their fish around as they sing the song below.

Tune: "Bicycle Built for Two"

Fishy, Fishy, swimming across the sea,
How I wish he'd swim right here to me.
We'd swish and swirl and swiggle,
And laugh and play and giggle.
Oh how I wish
That wiggly fish
Would swim right here to me.

Variation:
Make other sea creatures (octopus, eel, sea horse, turtle) in a similar manner. Use their names in the song.

This activity also helps children learn about:
expressive language.

Dear Parents,

One way children learn about language is by listening to it. They absorb new vocabulary by hearing words used again and again. They learn about beginning and ending sounds, sentence structure, grammar, and much more. Once they recognize letters, they begin to understand that words that start the same way—tooth, tall, tiny, Tuesday—all begin with the same letter, t. They start to "sound out" words.

Read to your child every day. She'll learn new words and new ideas from listening to stories. In addition to regular storybooks, ask your librarian to suggest books where the story is told in rhyme. Share some books of simple poetry.

Give your child opportunities to listen to the radio. Sing along with the radio or other recorded music, and sing simple songs together. This helps your child hear the rhythm of music and the rhyming sounds of many lyrics.

Listen to your child when she talks to you. When possible, stop what you are doing and make eye contact while you listen. For more listening fun, try the "Quick Trick" below:

A Quick Trick with Sounds

Gather These Materials:
none

Where: anywhere outdoors

How: Take a "listening walk" with your child down the street, in a park, or around the block to practice listening skills.

Stop walking, be very still, and listen for the sounds around you. Sometimes, closing your eyes helps you focus on what you hear. After 30 seconds, open your eyes and take turns telling each other the sounds you heard. After each person mentions a sound, be quiet and listen so the other person can hear and identify that sound, too.

DRAMATIC PLAY

Dramatic play gives your children an opportunity to use language in new ways. While pretending to be circus clowns, they may use silly words and phrases; as police officers they speak with authority and tell others what to do.

Children engage in dramatic play often. Join in their play from time to time to bring new vocabulary to it: "Officer Dan, did you arrest the suspect?"

Encourage all dramatic play that is safe, and you'll see your children's language skills grow.

Changing Roles
A Quick Trick with Action Figures or Small Toys

Gather These Materials:
favorite book
action figures or small beanbag toys

Where: anywhere

How: Read a favorite book with a small group of your children. Select action figures or small beanbag toys to represent characters in the story. These figures don't have to look exactly like the characters. You might have three small animal toys represent the Billy Goats Gruff and one action figure as the troll.

With the children, use the figures to act out the story. Don't worry about the dialog being exactly correct. At the story's end, change roles and act out the story again.

Variation:
Have your children make simple drawings of the story's characters. Have them cut out the drawings and glue them to cardboard, then, with your help, cut out the cardboard-backed figures. They can use these as characters for acting out stories.

This activity also helps children learn about:
taking turns in conversation.

Drama Cards
A Quick Trick with Index Cards, Pictures, and Stickers

Gather These Materials:
magazines and catalogs
scissors
glue
large index cards
stickers
markers

Where: anywhere

How: Have your children look in magazines and catalogs to help you find pictures of characters (child, adult, dinosaur, puppy) and settings (classroom, beach, jungle, castle, farm). Together, cut out these pictures and glue one to each index card. You can also use markers to draw cards and use stickers for characters (teddy bear, popular video characters, fish, animals). Sort the cards into two piles—characters and settings. Place the piles of cards face down.

   Have a child select one card from each pile and turn them face-up. Together, have the group discuss possible stories that could involve these cards. (A dragon at the beach might dance in the surf, have his fiery breath extinguished by the waves, or swim to his dentist to have her look at a loose tooth.) Encourage suggestions. Have a volunteer act out a situation you've created. The "act" can be as simple as one or two sentences. (While making swimming motions, a child might say, "Oh, my tooth is loose. I'd better swim to the dentist and let her check it!") If no one volunteers, demonstrate a way of acting out the story, and let the children copy your idea. Then have another child select new cards and continue the game until each child has selected cards.

Variation:
On index cards, draw simple faces that indicate emotions: happy, sad, angry, grumpy, afraid, and excited. To add a new element to the dramatic game, add this group of cards to the game.

This activity also helps children learn about:
expressing emotions.

Let's Pretend

A Quick Trick with Ourselves as Actors

Gather These Materials:
none

Where: anywhere

How: Children begin playing "Let's Pretend" by acting out things they know. "Let's pretend you're the Mommy and I just bumped my knee." Take turns with your children making up "Let's Pretend" activities. Act them out together. Keep the situations simple. Suggestions: "Let's pretend we are babies and we don't know how to walk." "Let's pretend it's cold and the wind is blowing, but we don't have our coats on." "Let's pretend we're eating soup that's very hot."

Variations:
Let the children offer suggestions for "Let's Pretend."
After your children have had practice recreating things they know, suggest pretend situations that require them to combine what they know with what they have not yet experienced. "Pretend you are driving a fire engine." "Let's pretend we are wiggly, just like gelatin." "Pretend the floor is very sticky and we are trying to walk on it." "Pretend we are working in the garden and the mosquitoes are biting us."

This activity also helps children learn about:
creative thinking.

Dressing Up
A Quick Trick with Clothing

Gather These Materials:
cast-off clothing
full-length mirror

Where: anywhere

How: From family donations or from garage sales, collect cast-off clothing. Allow your children to dress up in the items. Encourage them to admire themselves in the full-length mirror. Any kind of clothing will do as long as it is a few sizes (or more) larger than your children. Cut off bottoms of long clothing so youngsters will not trip on the items.

Look, too, for items like everyday shoes, dance shoes, hard hats, military hats, jewelry, scarves, plastic sunglasses, old eyeglasses without lenses, briefcases, and pocketbooks. When children put on other clothing, they also put on other identities and use other vocabulary. They may repeat scenes they've seen at home or on television, and they will make up new scenarios as well.

Don't be concerned if children try on clothing of the opposite sex. That's a healthy way to see the world from another point of view.

This activity also helps children learn about:
role playing.

Quick Tricks for Language ©2001 Monday Morning Books, Inc.

Making Costumes
A Quick Trick with Familiar Items

Gather These Materials:
scarves
safety pins
mittens and a knitted hat
other everyday items

Where: anywhere

How: Pin two adjacent corners of a square scarf to the shoulders of a child's shirt, and he instantly becomes a caped super-hero. In mittens and a knitted hat, he might become a frosty snowman or an Arctic explorer.

 Have your children think of other items that can help transform them into other characters. Encourage children to use appropriate words for the characters they have become. "I've come to save the day. I'll banish the scary dragons."

Variation:
Provide 12-inch by 18-inch (30-cm by 45-cm) pieces of construction paper for the children to use for making a simple crown. Fasten the crowns with paper clips. Have the children choose bath towels to drape around their shoulders for regal robes, and wrap aluminum foil around cardboard, paper towel tubes for scepters. They are now rulers of their own domains.

This activity also helps children learn about:
how one thing can represent another.

Prop Boxes
A Quick Trick with Collections of Props

Gather These Materials:
everyday items (see below)
commercially prepared toys
storage boxes

Where: gather items anywhere
put finished boxes where children can safely reach them

How: Gather a number of props around a particular theme. For example, at a fast food restaurant, you might gather a place mat, napkin, cup, and a French fry container. Encourage the children to use these in their play and to talk about what they are doing. When they are through playing with the items, store them in a box that has the restaurant's logo on the outside.

Variation:
Gather items to make a number of prop boxes. A few suggestions:
    Doctor/Nurse: Band-Aids, gauze, plastic medicine dropper, toy thermometer, toy syringe, craft sticks/tongue depressors
    Office worker: paper, pencils, paper clips, clipboard, small stapler and staples, memo pad
    Cook/Chef: pots, pans, spoons, egg beater, plastic plates, bowls, cups, saucers, tumblers, empty food packages
    Grocery store clerk: empty food packages, grocery bags, toy cash register (optional), pencils, paper, basket for groceries

This activity also helps children learn about:
the jobs of people in the community.

Moving to Music
A Quick Trick with Music

Gather These Materials:
musical tapes or CDs

Where: anywhere

How: Play music and ask the children to move the way the music suggests. Use a variety of tempos and moods: classical, marches, jazz, new age, gospel, country and western, music from other countries, soundtracks from movies. Accept any safe movements the children create, even if they are moving differently from the way you might move to that music.

Ask each child who or what would move the way he is moving: A soldier? A bunny? A floating cloud? A tree in the wind? Encourage the child to tell you more.

Variation:
Ask the group to describe each child's movements. Accept all answers from one-word responses to full sentences.

This activity also helps children learn about:
attentive listening.

News Reporter
A Quick Trick with a Tube and Aluminum Foil

Gather These Materials:
tubes from paper towels, 1 for each child
aluminum foil
permanent marker (supervise carefully)

Where: anywhere

How: Help your children cover tubes with aluminum foil. Don't worry about neatness. Tell your children the aluminum-covered tubes are microphones. Supervise carefully while you have each child put letters or a number (for TV/radio call letters or TV channel numbers) on his microphone.

Take a microphone and, talking into it, introduce yourself as a reporter for a local station. Think of a situation familiar to the children, and begin reporting on that. "We're here on Halifax Avenue to talk with people who ate at a restaurant last night. What is your name, young man?" Hold the microphone toward a boy for his answer. Ask about the restaurant, what he liked best, and whether he'd like to eat there again. Now give him the "microphone" and let him choose a child to interview. After two or three children have interviewed each other in front of the group, let all of them use their microphones to interview each other.

Variation:
Begin a story about children who worked with building blocks (or whatever the children are playing with currently). Using the "microphone" and prefacing the questions with a TV-type introduction of the children, ask questions about that activity. "What are you building? How many blocks do you think you'll need?"

This activity also helps children learn about:
taking turns in conversation.

Quick Tricks for Language ©2001 Monday Morning Books, Inc.

Pass the Mask
A Quick Trick with Imagination

Gather These Materials:
none

Where: anywhere you can see each other

How: Sit so everyone can see each other. Talk about feelings for a minute or two. Then tell your children you are going to play a game that shows how feelings might look and that you will pass that look from person to person. Have a child name a feeling such as fear, sadness, joy, or surprise. Make a face that expresses that feeling and "freeze" it on your face like a mask. Pretend to peel off the mask from top to bottom and pass it to someone else in the group. That person pretends to put on the mask for everyone to see. Pass the mask in turn to others in the group.

Variation:
Repeat the activity with each person in the group having a turn to name a feeling and a turn to be first to show the feeling.

This activity also helps children learn about:
identifying feelings.

Telephone Manners
A Quick Trick with a Telephone

Gather These Materials:
discarded telephones with cords removed or toy telephones
cardboard tube or other prop for another telephone

Where: anywhere

How: Have a child "call you" using a discarded or toy telephone. Pick up another telephone to "answer" the call. When you "answer" the call, model the correct way to answer a phone. Help children learn to ask politely for the person they wish to speak with, to talk into the receiver, and hang up politely when the conversation is finished.

   Now, "call" individual children and help them learn polite responses for answering the phone. Discuss what they should say and do if the caller asks to speak to someone else in the family.

Variation:
After your children learn telephone etiquette, help each make a small book of classmates' telephone numbers. (Ask parents' permission before distributing children's phone numbers.) Remind parents to always supervise when their young children use the telephone.

This activity also helps children learn about:
vocabulary.

Hello. May I speak with...

What If?

A Quick Trick with Familiar Stories

Gather These Materials:
familiar storybooks

Where: anywhere

How: After reading a familiar story, talk with your children in a play-ful way about other possibilities in the story. Ask questions like these: "What if the smallest Billy Goat (in "The Three Billy Goats Gruff") had given the troll a big picnic basket of food to eat? What do you think would have happened next?" Encourage and accept any answers. Ask a few more "what if" questions about the story, then encourage the children to ask you "what if" questions.

Variation:
After reading "Goldilocks and the Three Bears," ask your children, "What if Goldilocks had swept the floor, washed the dishes, made the beds, and then left before the bears came home?" "What if the Bears' door had been locked and Goldilocks couldn't get in the house?"

This activity also helps children learn about:
creative thinking.

Dear Parents,

Children learn language skills when they act out scenarios and when they pretend to be other people. They practice new vocabulary while they are acting. Pretending encourages them to use creative thinking skills. You can encourage this kind of play by letting your child "dress up" in your shoes, hats, and scarves or letting him use household items while playing. With pots and pans, he can pretend to be a restaurant cook. Putting a sheet over a table creates a house, cave, or hideaway underneath for dramatic play.

Acting out things your child remembers from the past relies on thinking skills and helps with language growth. Try the "Quick Trick" below to spark this kind of memory play.

A Quick Trick with Photographs

Gather These Materials:
family photographs

Where: anywhere

How: Together, look through snapshots of activities that included your child. Talk about the events in the photos and reenact them in an informal way. "Remember when we went to the park and you chased the butterfly? Let's pretend we are doing that now." "Remember when it rained and rained? Show me how we put on our rain boots. What happened next? Show me how you ran in the rain. How did I look when I ran in the rain?"

LEARNING VOCABULARY

Children have opportunities to learn vocabulary every time they hear spoken words used in meaningful ways. Reading books, singing songs, listening to songs and poetry, and playing games are fun ways to learn vocabulary.

Take advantage of the many opportunities you have to talk informally with your children. If they are helping you put away toys, talk about the toys and where they go. Talk about what you are doing when you help them put on coats and shoes.

Talk to the children while they are playing with blocks, puzzles, magnets, puppets, and games. Enter into their play from time to time, and ask questions that cannot be answered with a simple "yes" or "no." Remember that a child's vocabulary triples between age three and age six. Give your children ample opportunities to learn and use new words every day.

People Watching
A Quick Trick with People

boy, striped shirt blue pants

Gather These Materials:
none

Where: anywhere there are people

How: While you and a few children are sitting together in a busy area, focus their attention on people who are there or passing by. Describe one person in simple terms (boy, striped shirt, blue pants) and see if the children can find that person. Repeat this a few times, then have each child, in turn, describe someone for you to find.

Variation:
Describe things that you can see and have the children find them from the descriptions. On some occasions, you might look for things in specific categories—plants, things larger than a lunch box, things that are soft, and so on.

This activity also helps children learn about:
listening skills.

Boy?

Alvin Ant
A Quick Trick with Tissue Paper and Pipe Cleaners

Gather These Materials:
black tissue paper, 1/2 sheet per child
black pipe cleaners or chenille stems
scissors
red construction paper
glue

Where: at a table

How: Have children crumple their tissue paper into an egg-shaped wad. These will become the ants. Have each child wrap one pipe cleaner around the "ant" about one-third of the way from one end of the egg shape to form a head. The ends of this pipe cleaner become two legs. Wrap two pipe cleaners one-third of the way from the other end of the egg shape. These will form the ant's abdomen and thorax, and the ends of these pipe cleaners will become four legs.

Have each child cut two circular shapes from the red paper and glue them on the head for eyes.

While singing the song below, have your children move Alvin around their bodies, describing in song where Alvin is going:

Tune: "The Bear Went over the Mountain"

Alvin Ant's crawling <u>up my arm</u>.
Alvin Ant's crawling <u>up my arm</u>.
Alvin Ant's crawling <u>up my arm</u>.
Where will he go from here?

With your children, take turns making up verses using location words and names of body parts (through my fingers, over my head, around my wrist). Alvin might also crawl under the table, over a chair, behind the book, and so on.

Variation:
Children can sing the song using small action figures or small stuffed animals, substituting their figure's name for "Alvin Ant."

This activity also helps children learn about:
names of body parts.

Bath Time
A Quick Trick with a Washcloth

Gather These Materials:
washcloths for each child

Where: anywhere

How: Give each child a washcloth. Have your children pretend they are taking a bath. First they climb into imaginary bathtubs, then they wash body parts as they are mentioned in the poem below. Let children in turn suggest names of body parts to substitute for the underlined word. Repeat the poem saying and bathing a different body part each time. If desired, sing the poem to the tune of "Twinkle, Twinkle Little Star."

> Bubble, bubble,
> Dirt is gone.
> In my tub,
> I wash my <u>chin</u>.

Variation:
Have each child, in turn, point to a body part and ask the remaining children to name the part before singing the next verse.

This activity also helps children learn about:
listening to follow directions.

A Better Way
A Quick Trick with Classroom Toys

Gather These Materials:
a few classroom toys

Where: anywhere

How: Tell the children a simple story about a fictional child who was playing with a toy and another who came and grabbed it away from him. Discuss ways to "use words" to settle such a situation. Choose two children to act out the story. You may need to tell them in detail what to say:

First child: "May I please have that truck? I need it for my parking lot."

Second child: "I'm using it now. I'll give it to you when I'm through."

In another acting out of the same story, the first child may grab the truck and the second may say, "Please give me back that truck. I'm playing with it. You can have it when I am through."

In another acting out, the first child may ask for the truck and the second may negotiate: "You can have this truck if you give me the fire truck to play with."

Variation:
Have the children act out stories where they properly use the words "please," "thank you," and "you're welcome."

This activity also helps children learn about:
negotiating peaceful solutions to their problems.

Name the Clothing
A Quick Trick with Catalogs

Gather These Materials:
clothing catalogs or advertising pages

Where: anywhere

How: Sit side-by-side with a child and open a clothing catalog so both of you can see it. Mention a clothing item you see on the page, for example, "I see a red jacket." Have the child point to the item that matches the description. If the child cannot find the item, point to it and name it. When the child becomes proficient at finding the items, let her describe a clothing article she sees and have you find it.

Variation:
Talk about the various clothing items and discuss their uses. A child in a warm climate will know little about snow clothing, for example. Explain why some people wear boots and snowsuits. Discuss athletic wear when you see it: soccer clothes, football jerseys, baseball uniforms and socks, and so on.

This activity also helps children learn about:
how clothing protects our bodies.

Other Languages
A Quick Trick with Music

Gather These Materials:
records, tapes, or CDs of lullabies in many languages

Where: wherever you have rest or nap time

How: At rest or nap time, play recordings of lullabies in many languages. Your children will be able to identify all of them as "going to sleep" music, regardless of the language.

Variation:

Help your children learn to count in other languages. High school or college language teachers can teach you the right words and pronunciations. Also, people from other countries can help. Don't be shy about asking. People enjoy sharing their native languages with others.

This activity also helps children learn about:
the sounds of other languages.

Shapely Snacks
A Quick Trick with Food

Gather These Materials:
various foods in different shapes (see below)

Where: any place you eat snacks or meals

How: Plan a snack or a light meal around foods of only one shape. Let the children help you prepare the foods. Here are some suggestions:

Circles—round crackers, simple sandwich cut with a round cookie cutter, banana slices, pita bread, muffins, cookies, cucumber slices, thin carrot slices, small hamburger and bun.

Triangles—triangular crackers, triangular chips, bread and cheese slices cut into triangles, brownies or bar cookies cut into triangles.

Squares—brownies, sheet cake or bar cookies cut into squares, square crackers and graham crackers, sliced cheese cut into squares, luncheon meat cut into squares, meat loaf.

Rectangles—rectangular crackers and granola bars, whole graham crackers, cookie/brownie rectangles, sandwiches cut into rectangles, meat loaf.

Variation:
Name the shape and use the name of each food item as you touch it, use it, and eat it. Example: "Today we're eating circles of pita bread. We're each putting banana circles into our pita's pocket and adding cottage cheese from a circular bowl."

This activity also helps children learn about:
preparing their own foods.

Soft, Fluffy, and White
A Quick Trick with a Fluffy Rug

Gather These Materials:
soft, fluffy rug (like a bath rug)

Where: anywhere

How: Let your children take turns standing barefoot on a soft, fluffy rug. Help them think of all the words that describe it (*soft, fluffy, dry, white*). Have them tell things about the rug: "My toes can curl in it." "It tickles my feet." "We have a rug like this in our house."

Variation:
Repeat this activity with items your children are touching with their hands: smooth paper, rough paper, bath towels, ice cubes, dolls, pillows, and more. Write the words your children use to describe the items. Read the words together from time to time.

This activity also helps children learn about:
properties of things.

soft, fluffy, dry, white

Things in the House
A Quick Trick with a House and Its Items

Gather These Materials:
none

Where: anywhere

How: Take your children on a simple field trip into a house, apartment, or mobile home. When you are in a room of the dwelling, talk about the name of the room. Have the children take turns pointing to an object in the room for others to name. In turn, have each child name an item in the room and have the others point to the item.

Variation:
When you see illustrations of rooms in picture books, talk about the rooms and what is in them. ("Goldilocks and the Three Bears" usually shows a kitchen, living room, and bedroom. "Little Red Riding Hood" shows Grandmother's bedroom.)

This activity also helps children learn about:
the variety of types of rooms and furniture.

Vegetable Prints
A Quick Trick with Fresh Vegetables

Gather These Materials:
paper towels
several shallow pans (disposable ones work well)
tempera paint in several colors
knife, for adult use only
fresh vegetables: celery, bell pepper, onion, head of cabbage
and lettuce, cauliflower and broccoli florets, carrot
plain paper

Where: at a table

How: Place a pad of paper towels in each pan. Pour a different color of paint over each pad, saturating the pad. Cut vegetables in a way that shows their form: cut celery, carrot, bell pepper, and onion cross-wise; cut a wedge of cabbage or lettuce. Show your children how to press the cut side of a vegetable onto the paint-filled pad and then touch the painted side onto the plain paper to leave a vegetable print.

Talk about the vegetables and their names while the children are making prints. Label each print on the paper with the name of the vegetable that left the print.

Variation:
Use sponges instead of paper towels.

This activity also helps children learn about:
how fresh vegetables and fruits smell.

Five Little Kittens
Quick Trick with Stickers and Index Cards

Gather These Materials:
6 index cards
5 cat stickers
1 dog sticker

Where: on the floor

How: Affix one sticker to each index card. Spread the cat cards on the floor in front of the children. Beginning at the children's left, count the cats with them. Have one child, sitting nearby, hold the dog card. Recite the following verse touching each cat in turn. At the next-to-last line, have the child with the dog card move the dog toward the cats and say, "Bow, wow, wow." As the dog barks, sweep the cats up in your hand and "hide" them behind your back.

> Five little kittens were playing on the floor.
> The first one said, "Let's hide behind the door."
> The second one said, "Let's play in the hall."
> The third one said, "I want to play ball."
> The fourth one said, "Let's scamper down the stairs."
> The fifth one said, "Let's play beneath the chairs."
> Along came a puppy dog—"Bow, wow, wow."
> Five little kittens are hiding right now.

Make the materials available for the children to play with so they can practice using ordinal numbers.

Variation:
Instead of stickers and index cards, use commercially available precut paper shapes.

This activity also helps children learn about:
counting as they count the kittens at the beginning of the activity.

Dear Parents,

Children can learn vocabulary every time they hear words used in meaningful ways. Reading books, singing songs, listening to songs and poetry, and playing games are fun ways to learn vocabulary.

Talk to your child when you are together. If she is helping you in the kitchen, talk about the foods you are preparing. Talk about the pots and pans and storage containers. Let your child help you set the table and put unbreakable items away after they are washed and dried. Talk about where these items go.

Talk about what you are doing when you help her dress. Name the body parts you are washing at bath time, and name the foods you are eating at mealtimes.

Examine fruits and vegetables at the market. Learn the names of the different kinds of produce. Try a new one from time to time to learn how it tastes. Talk about your discoveries. Remember that a child's vocabulary triples between age three and age six. Give your child ample opportunities to learn new words every day.

Learning should never be a chore. The "Quick Trick" below offers a way for your child to learn words while playing a game with you.

A Quick Trick with Memories

Gather These Materials:
none

Where: anywhere

How: Play a guessing game with your child. Describe someone she knows well and challenge her to guess the person's identity.

Quick Tricks for Language ©2001 Monday Morning Books, Inc.

EMERGENT READING:
LETTER RECOGNITION TRICKS

Learning to read is a process that unfolds over time. First children learn to hear language, then to speak it. Children who are read to and who see adults reading and writing become interested in the "squiggly marks" they see on paper. They begin to realize that these things called letters carry important meaning.

Once this interest is kindled, the children enjoy playing with three-dimensional letters, tracing them, feeling them, and moving them around. First, they match them by their shapes. Over time, they learn the names of the letters.

Sticky Letters
A Quick Trick with Magnetic Letters

Gather These Materials:
magnetic plastic letters

Where: on any magnetic surface—refrigerator, file cabinet, metal cookie sheets

How: Put the letters in alphabetical order on a magnetic surface. With your children, sing the "Alphabet Song" very slowly, pointing at each letter as you say its name.

Variation:
Spread out the magnetic letters at random near the magnetic surface. Encourage your children, in turn, to place the letters on the surface, in order, as together you sing the "Alphabet Song" very slowly. If a child needs help finding a letter, use language to give clues. ("The M is green. It's beside a yellow O." "The F is under a purple K.")

This activity also helps children learn about:
the sequence of letters in the alphabet.

Magnetic Name
A Quick Trick with Lids

Gather These Materials:
100 adhesive-backed labels
100 same-size lids from cans of frozen juice
permanent marker
magnetic tape (available at hardware stores)

Where: on a refrigerator door, a metal cookie sheet, the side of a filing cabinet, or any other magnetic surface.

How: Place a label on each lid. Writing one uppercase letter on each lid, make three sets of alphabet lids (78 lids). Use the extra lids to make more vowel lids (A, E, I, O, U, Y). Cut 1-inch (2.5-cm) pieces of magnetic tape. Peel the backing off the tape and press a strip of the magnetic tape onto the back of each juice can lid.

   Sit at a magnetic surface with a child. From the lids, select two each of the letters that make up his name. Place the lids at random on the magnetic surface. Encourage the child to "find the ones that are the same and put them together." (Don't worry about the letters being in order.) Repeat the activity at other times with each of your children.

Variation:
Help the child put one set of letters in order to spell his name. Now have him arrange the other set below the first so they match. Name the letters as he puts them in order.

This activity also helps children learn about:
visual discrimination.

Quick Tricks for Language ©2001 Monday Morning Books, Inc.

In the News

A Quick Trick with a Newspaper

Gather These Materials:
index cards, cut into thirds
old newspapers
markers

Where: at a table or on the floor

How: Write capital letters on the cut-up index cards, one letter per card piece. Give your children markers and old newspapers. Have each child choose a letter card. Challenge children to look at the newspaper headlines to find the letters that match those on their cards. Have them circle the letters when they find them. Now have them select another card and continue the game.

Variation:
Write both the capital letter and the lowercase letter on each card and let the children look for and circle all that they find.

This activity also helps children learn about:
finding information on a page, a skill used in looking up words in a dictionary or numbers in a phone book.

Watch the Letters I
A Quick Trick with Plastic Letters

Gather These Materials:
plastic letters
cookie sheet or large piece of cardboard

Where: at a table

How: Place three letters on the table in front of you so that every-one playing the game can see them. Have the children look care-fully at the letters and name them. Place the cookie sheet be-tween the letters and the children so the children cannot see the letters.

Remove one of the letters and hide it behind you or in your lap. Remove the cookie sheet so the children can see the remaining letters. Have them guess which letter is gone.

Repeat with other letters. As the children's skill increases, use four letters at a time.

Variation:
Do the same activity using numerals in place of letters.

This activity also helps children learn about:
focusing their attention.

Quick Tricks for Language ©2001 Monday Morning Books, Inc.

Watch the Letters 2
Another Quick Trick with Plastic Letters

Gather These Materials:
plastic letters
cookie sheet or large piece of cardboard

Where: at a table

How: Place three letters on the table in front of you so that everyone playing the game can see them. Have the children look carefully at the letters and name them. Place the cookie sheet between
the letters and the children so the children cannot see the letters.
Remove one letter and replace it with another that has been hiding
in your lap. Remove the cookie sheet and have the children tell you
what is different.

Variation:
As your children's skill increases, play with four letters. Remove
and replace one letter.

This activity also helps children learn about:
increasing their powers of observation.

Eating Letters
A Quick Trick with Letter-Shaped Cereal

Gather These Materials:
letter-shaped breakfast cereal
small bowl

Where: at a table

How: Pour some letter-shaped cereal into a small bowl. Have your children wash their hands. Have them, in turn, take a letter from the bowl and identify the letter. If a child is unable to identify a letter, let the group help. Let the children eat their letters after they are named.

Variation:
Make the letter-shaped cereal available for children to explore. Some will form their names or copy words they see around them. Others may look for matching letters.

This activity also helps children learn about:
visual discrimination.

Quick Tricks for Language ©2001 Monday Morning Books, Inc.

EMERGENT READING:
WORD RECOGNITION TRICKS

As children become familiar with letters, they begin to realize that when letters are put together, they make words. When a child asks how to make a particular word, use the movable letters to make the word. Say each letter as you put it in place, then encourage the child to say the letters with you as you both point to them, in order, from left to right.

After many experiences with this method, write the word on an index card for the child to copy using the movable letters. Encourage children to keep their word cards in a safe place so they can use them again and again.

Labels
A Quick Trick with Index Cards

Gather These Materials:
scissors
index cards
pen
masking tape

Where: in your classroom

How: Cut the index cards lengthwise into thirds yielding strips 1 inch by 5 inches (2.5 cm by 12.5 cm). On each strip, write the name of something in the room: door, window, chair, floor, table. Show your children one label, and tell them what it says. Let them help you tape the label to the correct item. Hang no more than six labels.

Ask a child to show you the label that says "door," for example. Repeat with the remaining labels. Touch a label and ask the children to tell you what it says. Repeat with the remaining labels. Encourage the children to ask each other what the labels say.

Variation:
After the labels have been in place a few days, add three more. Let your children suggest items to be labeled. Continue adding labels in this manner, a few each time.

This activity also helps children learn about:
decoding words by noticing the order of the letters.

Letter Carrier
A Quick Trick with Baskets and Envelopes

Gather These Materials:
marker
index cards
hole punch
pipe cleaners or chenille stems
baskets, 1 for each child
envelopes
adhesive-backed labels (optional)
several purses or briefcases

Where: at a table

How: Preparation: Use a marker to write each child's name on a different index card. Let your children help you punch a hole in the center of the top of each card and use a pipe cleaner to attach each card to a different basket. These are the baskets for incoming mail. Address envelopes with the names of the children in your class. Make several for each person. (You can reuse envelopes from "junk" mail by putting a label on each one and writing a different child's name on each label.)

Activity: Divide the "incoming mail" and put some in each purse or briefcase. Distribute the purses to children, and show them how they can "deliver" the mail to the correct baskets by matching the names on the envelopes to the names on the baskets. Be sure every child has an opportunity to deliver mail.

Variation:
Take your children to the post office to mail letters to themselves. Arrange beforehand for the children to have a brief "behind the scenes" tour to see where mail is sorted and loaded on mail trucks.

This activity also helps children learn about:
sorting and matching.

Quick Tricks for Language ©2001 Monday Morning Books, Inc.

My Colorful Garden
A Quick Trick with a Flower/Seed Catalog

Gather These Materials:
scissors
flower or seed catalogs
basket
various-color markers
stick-on labels for file folders
large piece of brown paper

Where: at a table

How: Let your children help you cut flowers from flower or seed cata-logs. Place the cutout pictures into a basket. Use the markers to write one color name on each stick-on label. Match the marker color to the color name—write "red" with a red marker, "orange" with an orange marker, and so on.

Draw widely spaced parallel lines on the large brown paper. This paper represents the not-yet-planted garden and the lines are the rows to plant the seeds. Stick one label at the end of each parallel line to show what color of flower will be planted in that row.

Show the children that the garden will have one row of red flow-ers, one row of orange, one row of purple, and so on. One at a time, have the children choose a flower cutout and then look at the "garden" to determine where to place the flower. Some children will match their flower color to the color of the printed word. Others will respond to the printed word itself. Most will use both clues together. When children have finished playing the game, put it in the room where they can later play independently.

Variation:
Glue the flowers into rows according to color. Use strips cut from index cards to write the color names as above. Have children match the index cards to the correct row of flowers in the garden.

This activity also helps children learn about:
matching and sorting.

Our Grocery Store
A Quick Trick with Empty Packages

Gather These Materials:
empty food packages
empty toiletry packages (toothpaste, lotion)
empty grocery bags
index cards
pens/markers

Where: in a corner of the room

How: Help your children set up a simple grocery store in a corner of the room. Give them empty, unbreakable food packages that one might find in a grocery store. (<u>Do not use glass</u> jars or bottles, and <u>be certain that cans have no sharp edges</u>.) Show the children how to find the name of each product. They may "read" the labels by looking at the pictures on them or by recognizing particular kinds of packages. Eventually, they will begin to recognize the printed words on the labels.

Each shopper can use an empty grocery bag to gather desired items. Use the index cards to label areas of the store: "Cold things," "Pasta," "Soup." Help children place the packages in the right areas.

When most of the groceries have been purchased, restock the store (by having shoppers return their purchases), and let the shopping begin again. Encourage shoppers and cashiers to name and talk about the items they are handling.

Variation:
Add the store ads from the food section of your newspaper. Encourage children to find foods in their store that match the foods in the ads.

This activity also helps children learn about:
sorting.

Quick Tricks for Language ©2001 Monday Morning Books, Inc.

Paper Dolly
A Quick Trick with Paper Dolls

Gather These Materials:
paper dolls (commercially produced or home-made)
paper-doll clothes
index cards
pen

Where: at a table

How: Cut the index cards into 1-inch by 5-inch (2.5-cm by 12.5-cm) strips. Provide your children with paper dolls and paper-doll clothing. On each index-card strip, write the name of a body part you can see on the dolls or a name of the various pieces of clothing the dolls have (leg, arm, foot, nose, red sweater, blue pants, boots).

Have your children, in turn, select a word card. Together, read the word aloud and have the child point to the correct body part or clothing article.

Variation:
For children who are beginning to read, display a paper doll and three word cards with body part names. Name (or point to) a body part on the doll. (This should match one of the displayed words.) Challenge a child to point to the correct word. Use words that begin with different letters so children can "sound out" the word and find it by looking for the correct beginning letter.

This activity also helps children learn about:
vocabulary for body parts and clothing.

Sew-and-Sew
A Quick Trick with a Paper Plate and Logos

Gather These Materials:
labels with logos from familiar products
scissors
glue
plain paper plates
hole punch
yarn
masking tape

Where: preparation—at a table
activity —anywhere

How: Have your children help you collect logos from familiar products: can labels, package labels, magazine ads, and newspaper ads. Together, cut out these logos and glue them, one each, to plain paper plates. After the glue dries, use a hole punch to punch holes around the rim of each plate, about 1 inch (2.5 cm) apart. Each plate becomes a sewing card.

For each plate, cut an 18-inch (45-cm) length of yarn. Wrap one end of the yarn with a short piece of masking tape (any width). This strengthens the end of the yarn and serves as a sewing "needle." Tie the other end of the yarn to a hole in the plate. Show the children how to sew by putting the needle through a hole and pulling the yarn gently until the free length comes through the hole. Show them how to sew up from beneath and back down in another hole. Encourage them to sew around the edge of the plate. Remember, they are beginners and they may sew across the plate and back, tangling the yarn. Help them remove the tangles and encourage them to begin again.

Ask the children to show you the plate that says "Zesty Toothpaste," "Ready-to-Go Pizza," or "Happy Burger." (Substitute the names of the logos on your plates.)

Variation:
Ask each child to identify the logo on the plate he is sewing. Sew with the children and ask them to identify the logo on your plate, as well.

This activity also helps children learn about:
increasing hand-eye coordination while sewing.

Parties and Holidays
A Quick Trick with Party Paper Goods

Gather These Materials:
paper cups, plates, and napkins with party themes

Where: on the floor

How: Collect leftover party plates, napkins, and cups with holiday or party greetings on them: Happy Holidays, Happy Birthday, 50th Anniversary, Congratulations, and so on. If possible, have a plate, napkin, and cup for each word pattern. Mix up the collection and give one or more items to each child. Ask the children to show you an item they might see at a birthday party or one that has a 5 on it, for example.

    Challenge the children to put together the items that go together. They will use colors and illustrations to help with the match, but over time will also become familiar with the words. Let your children use the items in their dramatic play.

Variation:
Include some items with no letters on them. Ask a child to find the ones with no writing and tell you what they might be used for (beach party or picnic, for example). This helps children develop the emergent reading skill of gaining information from context cues.

This activity also helps children learn about:
sorting and matching.

Please Read to Me
A Quick Trick with Storybooks and a Tape Recorder

Gather These Materials:
tape cassettes
cassette tape recorder
storybooks

Where: anywhere

How: Before you read to your children, place a blank tape cassette in a recorder and set the recorder nearby. Set it to record while you are reading aloud to your children. Read slowly and say "turn the page" just as you turn each page. Wait a moment after turning each page before beginning to read again.

Rewind the tape, and show the children how to use the recorder. Now they can listen to you reading to them even when you are unable to do so. Encourage them to follow along in the book, turning the page when they hear that message.

Record every time you read, and you'll soon have a library of tapes for your children to use and enjoy.

Variation:
Have other familiar people record books for the children: another teacher, parents, school director, or bus driver, for example.

This activity also helps children learn about:
listening.

Quick Tricks for Language ©2001 Monday Morning Books, Inc.

Reading Signs
A Quick Trick with Signs

Gather These Materials:
none

Where: on a walk, in the school bus

How: Take a walk with your children to a place where they can see a traffic sign, like a stop sign. If it's safe to do so, go close to the sign and lift the children one at a time so they can touch the letters and feel the sign. Talk about the sign's colors, its shape, and the letters on it. Tell the children what the sign says and point out the letters that make up the word. Explain what the sign is for and why it is there. Make a replica of the sign to hang in your room where the children can study it. Repeat this activity on other days with other signs.

When you are in the school bus with your children, point out similar signs as you pass them. Introduce only one sign at a time to avoid confusing the children.

Variation:
Use construction paper or cardboard to make small signs like those you've seen. Let your children use them in play. They may want to set up a roadway for small cars and trucks and use the signs with that.

This activity also helps children learn about:
reasons for written words.

Card Game
A Quick Trick with a Gift Bag

Gather These Materials:
toy ads
scissors
glue or glue sticks
index cards
marker
gift bag

Where: preparation—at a table
activity—anywhere

How: Give your children advertisements for toys and toy stores. Have them cut out pictures of some of their favorite toys and glue one picture on each index card. Let them tell you the names of the toys so you can print each name on the appropriate index card.

Have the children mix up the cards and put them in the gift bag. In turn, have each child take one card from the bag and "read" the name of the toy. Children will use the pictures as clues, but over time they will read the words.

Variation:
Repeat the activity on other days using labeled pictures of other categories of items: colors, numerals and number names, foods, furniture, kitchen items, or animals, for example.

This activity also helps children learn about:
using context clues to help identify words.

Word Bank
A Quick Trick with Index Cards and Shoe Boxes

Gather These Materials:
crayons/markers
index cards
shoe box for each child

Where: at a table

How: Have your children draw pictures of some of their favorite things, one item per card. (Many will draw what they are able to draw, not necessarily their "favorites". That's acceptable, too.) Beside each picture, write the name of the item: rainbow, Daddy, swing, tree, Adventure Man, Cinderella. The cards become the treasure of the child who drew them.

Have each child decorate a shoe box as a bank or treasure box. Have the children put their word card "treasures" in their banks. Ask the children to read their own word cards to you from time to time. Encourage them to draw more pictures on other days so they can add to their collections.

Have the children read their cards to each other or to other adults. Have them show their cards to each other. They may want to copy each others' cards. Encourage this activity because children learn new words from this exposure.

Variation:
Invite the children to cut and paste magazine, advertising, and catalog pictures to illustrate some of their cards.

This activity also helps children learn about:
nouns and how a written word can represent a person, place, or thing.

Dear Parents,

Learning to recognize letters is an early step in learning to read. The first letter in a child's name is usually the first letter he learns to recognize and name. Over time, children become familiar with other letters that are important to them.

When you are reading together, point out to your child the first letter of his name. When he learns that thoroughly, point out other letters. Do this, also, when you pass road and store signs while riding in a car or bus. Soon he will recognize whole words.

Surround your child with printed words. Have magazines and books on hand to look at and for you to read together.

Provide your child with three-dimensional letters. Serve him alphabet soup and alphabet-shaped cereals so he can "eat" letters and can make and "eat" words. Help him identify the letters or words he is eating. Over time your child will learn all of the letter.

Have fun while you explore letters. Try the "Quick Trick" below to add to your letter-identification fun:

A Quick Trick with Pancakes

Gather These Materials:
pancake batter
frying pan
spatula
breakfast plate

Where: in the kitchen

How: Prepare pancake batter using your favorite recipe or a commercially made mix. When you pour the batter into the frying pan, slowly pour it in the shape of the first letter in your child's name. Cook as usual and then, using a spatula, serve the letter right-side-up on your child's plate. Talk about the letter and help your child name it. In time, he will request certain letters. Honor those requests.

When your child can identify many letters, make all of the letters of his name with pancake batter. Place the cooked pancakes in order on his plate so he can "read" his name.

EMERGENT WRITING:
LETTER FORMATION TRICKS

As children begin to recognize letters, they also start making "squiggles" of their own. As their small muscles become better coordinated, their writing begins to look like real letters. Support the children's actions when they use "writing" materials for making scribbling motions or drawing circles. Drills of making line after line of the same letter will thwart a child's enthusiasm for writing.

It's easier for children to begin forming letters with materials like modeling dough and finger paint. When children play with manipulative materials like modeling dough and beads and string, they strengthen their finger muscles and increase their hand-eye coordination.

Close Shave
A Quick Trick with Shaving Cream

Gather These Materials:
aerosol shaving cream (without added menthol)
cookie sheets, cafeteria trays, or large baking pans
damp towels

Where: at a table

How: For each child, squirt some shaving cream on a cookie sheet, tray, or large baking pan. Let your children use their fingers to practice forming letters and numerals in the shaving cream. Caution: Remind children not to rub their eyes or noses because their hands are covered with soap. Have damp towels nearby in case the soapy cream does get on faces.

Clean-up is easy. Just wipe the soapy surface with a squeegee or a damp sponge! Remind children they don't need to use soap to wash the shaving cream off their hands. The shaving cream is soap. They only need to rinse.

Variation:
Drop a few drops of food coloring onto the trays and have the children mix it into the shaving cream.

This activity also helps children learn about:
how letters "feel."

Sweet, Sweet Letters
A Quick Trick with Cookie Dough

Gather These Materials:
tablespoon
sugar cookie dough (a tube of commercially available
refrigerated dough is fine)
waxed paper
cookie sheet
oven

Where: at a table

How: Begin by having the children wash their hands. Place a
rounded tablespoon of chilled cookie dough on a piece of waxed
paper in front of each child. Show the children how to roll the ball
into a "snake" and how to use the snake to form simple letters.
Place the letters on the cookie sheet. Continue until all the dough
has been used. Help your children name the letters they form.
Bake the cookies according to recipe directions, but watch carefully. You may need to bake for more or less time than the directions suggest. When the cookies cool, help the children name the
letters as they eat them.

Variation:
Have your children use the dough to make numerals.

This activity also helps children learn about:
how things change when you cook them. Soft, pliable dough
becomes a firm cookie.

Quick Tricks for Language ©2001 Monday Morning Books, Inc.

Writing in the Snow
A Quick Trick with Fresh Snow

Gather These Materials:
water
"squirt" bottles (used for ketchup and mustard)
food coloring

Where: outdoors in snowy weather, where available

How: Have your children fill squirt bottles with water and add food coloring to each bottle, one color per bottle. When the children go outdoors to play, encourage them to use the squirt bottles to "draw" colored letters in the snow. Remember that children who are "just squirting here and there" are building muscles and coordination needed for writing. Reminder: If the children are not wearing water-proof mittens or gloves, place a plastic bag over their hands to protect them from the wet and cold.

Variation:
Children can write numerals with the squirt bottles.

This activity also helps children learn about:
hand-eye coordination.

Stamp It Out!
A Quick Trick with Rubber Stamps

Gather These Materials:
letter-shaped rubber stamps (available commercially)
stamp pads
plain paper (scrap paper is fine)

Where: at a table

How: Show your children another way to make letters. Demonstrate how to use the rubber stamps by pressing them against the stamp pad and then pressing them against the paper. Let the children explore and use the materials. From time to time, help your children identify the letters they have used. Children who are ready may try forming their names or other words that are important to them.

Variation:
Show your children how they can use water color markers to color part of a letter stamp in one color and another part in a different color before stamping. If the color dries out on the stamp before stamping, have them gently exhale on the stamp then press it to the paper.

This activity also helps children learn about:
transferring color from one surface to another.

Pudding Practice
A Quick Trick with Pudding

Gather These Materials:
pudding prepared according to package directions (instant pudding works as well as the cooked varieties)
unbreakable baking pan or cookie sheet, 1 for each child

Where: at a table

How: Have the children wash their hands thoroughly before they begin this activity, then have each child put a heaping tablespoon of prepared pudding in an individual baking pan. Have the children use their fingers to "finger paint" in the pudding.

After they have explored the pudding a few minutes, challenge them to make letters. Most will start with the letters in their names. Suggest that they practice forming numerals in their pudding, too.

For children, part of the fun is the ease of "erasing" their efforts by dragging their hands through the pudding. Laugh with them when the letters disappear. Encourage the children to clean up by licking their hands and fingers. Follow up with thorough hand washing.

Variation:
Instead of a baking pan, place a large piece of waxed paper on the table in front of each child. Have children put two or three tablespoons of pudding on their paper before forming letters.

This activity also helps children learn about:
aromas and flavors.

EMERGENT WRITING: WORD FORMATION TRICKS

Children learn about words by "inventing" their own spelling. They may write I L M M for "I love Mommy," writing the predominant sounds they hear. Slowly this "spelling" becomes more and more precise. This is an authentic stage in writing and should be accepted and celebrated. "Correcting" pre-school children's attempts at spelling and composing frustrates their natural development of writing abilities. Be patient and encourage all attempts at writing and forming words.

Meeting the Tools
A Quick Trick with Writing Implements

Gather These Materials:
ballpoint pens of different colors
thick- and thin-point washable markers
pencils of different diameters
colored pencils
crayons
paper

Where: at a table

How: Give some of the writing implements listed above to your children to explore. Talk about the ways they feel and smell. Have children "write something" (make a few marks) on paper using two similar implements of different colors (red pencil and black pencil). Discuss how they are the same and different.

For each child, fold a paper in eighths, then unfold. Challenge your children to use different writing tools to "write something" (make marks, letters, pictures, or designs) in each section of the paper. Talk about the results. Which items make thick lines? Which make thin lines?

Variation:
Ask the children to describe to you any of the things they've written.

This activity also helps children learn about:
comparing things that are similar.

Writing Area
A Quick Trick with Scrap Paper

Gather These Materials:
baskets
scrap paper
memo pads
used envelopes (from incoming mail)
markers, pens, pencils, colored pencils

Where: at a child-size desk or table

How: Set up a "writing area" for your children. Provide a basket of scrap paper and memo pads, another basket of envelopes, and a basket full of writing implements. Encourage your children to use the supplies to write letters, notes, reports, recipes, menus, restaurant orders, and more. Some children may want to make paper money. Encourage all writing efforts.

Ask the children to "read".you the things they've written or to tell you about them.

Variation:
For older children, add simple picture books to this area. Encourage the children to copy words or a sentence from the picture book. Compliment all efforts.

This activity also helps children learn about:
sorting and organizing items at a desk.

Remember This
A Quick Trick with Message Pads

Gather These Materials:
pencils
memo pads of many kinds

Where: anywhere

How: Let your children see you writing messages to yourself: a grocery list, telephone messages, notes of things to tell to other adults, and "to-do" lists. Make pencils and pads available to the children. When you ask them to do something, encourage them to write themselves a note. (For example, you may tell one child to put away three things: the lion puppet, the lion puzzle, and the safari hat.) Whether they write "real words," make pictures, scribble, or make three marks on the paper, they will know what the note says, and the note will help them remember. If they later ask you what they were supposed to do, refer them to their notes.

Variation:
Help your children make short "to-do" lists of things they plan to do during the day. Show them how to cross off each item when they have finished doing the activity.

This activity also helps children learn about:
important reasons for writing.

Quick Tricks for Language ©2001 Monday Morning Books, Inc.

Making Lists
A Quick Trick with Paper and Markers

Gather These Materials:
markers
paper

Where: anywhere

How: Let your children see you making a list—of items on a shelf, of your favorite colors, of what you are wearing today, of your favorite books. Give the children paper and markers and have each of them make a list. Suggested topics: red things, favorite toys, names of friends, things that touch the floor, soft things, things with wheels. Use different topics on different days. Continue the activity until children begin to lose interest. Accept any kind of marks for the list: scribbling, pictures, or actual letters. Understanding that things can be written down is the important learning in this activity.

Variation:
Add a numeric slant to the list to reinforce math learning: "Make a list of four soft things." "List five foods you like to eat."

This activity also helps children learn about:
important reasons for writing.

Sign In, Please
A Quick Trick with Pencil and Paper

Gather These Materials:
a clipboard for each child (you can use pieces of
cardboard with paper clips for holding paper in place)
paper
pencil

Where: at a table

How: Your children have seen adults sign in at the doctor's
office, the hair-styling salon, busy restaurants, and other places.
Give each child a clipboard and tell the children that they
must sign in before taking out toys to play. Have them "write"
their names and "write" (or draw) the toy they will play with.
They can add to their sign-in sheets each time they take out
another item. Encourage them to mark the toys' names (or
pictures) with a check when they put the items away. After
play time, you can review the lists with your children and have
them tell you what they've played with.

Variation:
Before your children play with stuffed animals, action figures, or
baby dolls, have them help these characters "sign in" to play.

This activity also helps children learn about:
planning ahead.

Toy Sign In

Correspondence
A Quick Trick with Envelopes and Advertising Stamps

Gather These Materials:
plain paper
pencils, pens, markers, or other writing implements
envelopes
stamps used to advertise book clubs and music clubs
file folder labels (optional)

Where: at a table

How: Give your children some paper and a pencil or marker and encourage them to write letters to family members and friends. Supply them with envelopes (used ones work fine) and advertising stamps so they can put their letters into envelopes and add stamps. If you provide used envelopes, give children some file folder labels so they'll have a clean surface to write the "address."

Accept any efforts children make to "write" or spell the addressees' names. If they ask you how to spell a word, write it on a scrap of paper for them to copy. Encourage children to deliver their mail to family members who live in their houses, to classmates, and to friends who they will see at home.

Variation:
Have your children draw pictures to send to family members and friends. Ask if they would like you to write their words on the pictures. Write them exactly as children say them, even if the grammar is incorrect. Have children put these pictures into envelopes as above and deliver the ones they can. Encourage parents to mail the ones that cannot be hand-delivered.

This activity also helps children learn about:
communicating with others through writing.

Phone Numbers
A Quick Trick with a Phone Book

Gather These Materials:
discarded phone books, 1 for each child
paper
pencil/marker

Where: at a table

How: Show a small group of children that the phone book contains many names and numbers. Show the ads section where they can find logos of their favorite restaurants and other familiar businesses: car lots, bakeries, motorcycle sales, and doll repair, for example. Give each child a phone book, paper, and marker. Let the children explore the books and copy down names and numbers at will. Repeat the activity with other small groups of children until everyone has had a turn.

Variation:
Provide discarded telephones (remove the cords) and encourage children to pretend to call the numbers they've recorded. Help them understand that they are not to do this activity with working telephones.

This activity also helps children learn about:
using a telephone book and telephone.

Quick Tricks for Language ©2001 Monday Morning Books, Inc.

Playing Author
A Quick Trick with a Storybook

Gather These Materials:
a favorite storybook
paper
pencils, pens, or markers

Where: at a table

How: When some of your children are forming letters with ease and have been attempting to "write real words," have each of them select a favorite picture book. Provide paper and pencils, pens, and markers. Encourage them to turn to any page in their book and copy some of the words they see. Do not do this with children who are not yet forming letters easily.

Variation:
Encourage your children to copy words and numerals from toy catalogs.

This activity also helps children learn about:
finding words in lots of places.

Dear Parents,

The children have been practicing writing at school. We've made letters out of various substances, like cookie dough, and we've written letters in shaving cream and in pudding. We've made letters with rubber stamps and have written lists with pencil and paper.

Some of us are still at the scribbling stage, and we want you to know that is normal. Writing takes a great deal of control in the small muscles of the hands. Some of us develop this control sooner than average, and some of us develop it later. But we will all develop the ability to guide a pencil.

Meanwhile, you can help your child practice writing by providing plenty of scrap paper along with markers, pencils, or crayons. The more your child scribbles and attempts to write, the more she will develop the small muscles necessary to write well. Don't rush this process and don't point out errors. Just provide the materials and keep it fun. The "Quick Trick" below will give you another idea for providing writing practice.

A Quick Trick with Powdered Drink Mix

Gather These Materials:
waxed paper
sweetened, powdered lemonade drink mix

Where: at a table

How: Put a large piece of waxed paper in front of your child. Have him spoon two tablespoons of powdered lemonade mix on the paper. Encourage your child to use his fingers to spread the mix and then to draw or write letters in it. When he begins to tire of the activity, he can "clean" his fingers by licking them. Have your child wash hands vigorously before and after this trick.

MAKING BOOKS

When children make their own books, they feel confident in "reading" them. There are endless ways to make books with children. The simplest is to gather and staple a few sheets of paper. You can add heavy paper front and back covers.

Other ideas include:

using colored papers for inside pages.

making book covers from wallpaper samples, wrapping paper, poster board, or large index cards.

decorating covers with magazine pictures, old greeting cards, stickers, rubber stamps, or markers.

cutting book pages and covers into shapes: mittens, bears, snowmen, triangles, circles, ovals, and so on.

fastening book pages and covers together with staples, paper fasteners, book rings, or yarn.

Cereal Book
A Quick Trick with Cereal Boxes

Gather These Materials:
empty cereal boxes
scissors
3-hole punch or any hole puncher
paper fasteners

Where: at a table

How: Ask parents to save empty cereal boxes and send them to school. Cut the boxes apart, saving the box fronts. Place the cereal box fronts face-down on a table and let each child choose a few of similar size for this activity. Help each child put his box fronts face-up and punch holes along the left edge of the box fronts. Have the children stack the fronts and fasten them together with the paper fasteners. Help each child "read" his book and then read it to another child. Let the children exchange and read each others' books.

Variation:
Let the children make books of other similar-size container fronts: pudding boxes, gelatin boxes, can labels, and so on.

This activity also helps children learn about:
how books are made.

Refrigerator Book
A Quick Trick with Food Pictures

Gather These Materials:
food ads
food labels
scissors
glue or glue sticks
12-inch by 18-inch (30-cm by 45-cm) paper, 1 sheet for each child
fine-line marker
2 sheets of 12-inch by 18-inch (30-cm by 45-cm) construction paper

Where: at a table

How: Save food ads and food labels. Have each child cut out three pictures of various foods that might go in the refrigerator and glue the pictures onto his sheet of paper. Let the children tell you the names of the foods so you can write the dictated words beside each picture using the fine-line marker.

Gather the pages, add construction paper covers, back and front, and staple the pages into book form. Write "The Refrigerator Book" on the book's cover and have a child draw a handle on the right-hand side of the refrigerator door cover. Now open the refrigerator and read about what is inside.

Variation:
Make an "Oven" book and let your children fill it with pictures of things that are cooked in an oven. Make a "Microwave Oven" book in the same manner.

This activity also helps children learn about:
sorting items that do and do not go into a refrigerator or other appliances.

My Favorite Food
A Quick Trick with Self-Made Books

Gather These Materials:
premade books containing 5 blank pages, 1 book for each child
markers or crayons

Where: at a table

How: Sing the song below, giving children, in turn, a chance to name their favorite food. On the last line, children pantomime eating the food. Change the underlined words in the song to reflect children's favorites.

Tune: "London Bridge"

Pizza (substitute child's choice) is my favorite food,
favorite food, favorite food.
Pizza is my favorite food,
Yum, yum, yummy.

Later, give each child a blank book. Have the children make pictures of their favorite foods, one food per page. Label the pictures with the names of the foods. Label each book "My Favorite Foods" and have the author/illustrator sign the cover. Sing the song again, following along in a book and substituting the foods on each page of the book for food names in the song. Over a few days, sing the song again and again until you've sung from every book.

Variation:
Use two paper plates as the front and back covers of each book. Cut round pages slightly smaller than the paper plates and bind the books by putting three equally spaced staples along one-quarter of the plates' edges.

This activity also helps children learn about:
recognizing the written names of foods.

Pizza is my favorite food.

Suitcase Book
A Quick Trick with a File Folder

Gather These Materials:
plain paper, 5 sheets for each child
file folders, 1 for each child
stapler and staples
magazines and catalogs
scissors
glue or glue sticks
pen
construction paper strips

Where: at a table

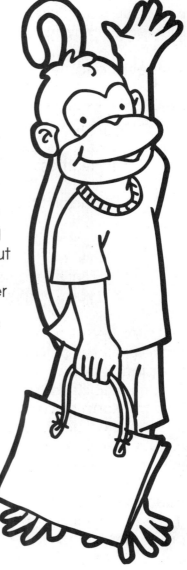

How: Preparation: For each child, place a stack of five sheets of plain paper inside a blank file folder. Turn the folder so the folded side is at the bottom and the open side is at the top. Staple about 1/4-inch (.6-cm) away from the edge along the bottom (folded) side of the file folder, forming a "suitcase book" with the file folder as the front and back cover and the blank papers as the pages.

In a large or small group, talk about traveling and the kinds of things people put in a suitcase when they take a trip. Discuss the different kinds and amounts of clothing you'd pack for a long summer vacation at a lake or seashore and for a weekend stay with Grandmom and Granddad.

Give your children magazines or catalogs and scissors. Have them cut out pictures of things they think they'd like to pack for an imaginary trip. Distribute the premade file folder books and show children how to turn them so that they become "suitcases." Let the children glue their pictures inside their individual suitcase books. Ask the children to tell you what word(s) to write beside each item. Have the children glue or staple paper strips to their folders to make the suitcases' handles. Take turns reading the suitcase books.

Variation:
Give your children a small suitcase to play with. Encourage their efforts to pack or unpack it, using real items. This gives them opportunities to use spoken language while talking about traveling, clothing, packing, and unpacking.

This activity also helps children learn about:
sorting items that go together.

Number Books
A Quick Trick with Crayons and Paper

Gather These Materials:
for each child, a premade book with 5 inside pages
markers or crayons

Where: at a table

In each premade book, write the numeral 1 on the first page, 2 on the second, and so on. Also write out the number names in full on each page: one, two, three, four, five. Give each child a numbered book. Have children draw one item on the first pages of their books, two matching items on the second, three matching items on the third, and so on. Label each page when the children tell you what is on that page—for example, one rainbow, two rings, three lollipops. Put a title on each book (Jan's Number Book) and let authors print their names on their covers. Ask the authors to read their books to you or to each other.

Variation:
Make books with more pages so your children can explore larger numbers.

This activity also helps children learn about:
number value.

Love Story
A Quick Trick with Discarded Valentines

Gather These Materials:
a premade book containing 4 pages, 1 book for each child
glue or glue sticks
discarded valentines

Where: at a table

How: Give your children the premade books and ask them to draw on each page a picture of someone they love. Have them dictate words for you to write on each picture. "I love my Granddaddy." "I love my brother, Patrick." Have each child glue a valentine on the front cover of his book. Write "I love…" on the front of each book. Let the authors print their names at the top of the front cover. Read the books to your children, then let them read their books to each other.

Variation:
Encourage children to make other "love" books—about pets, about foods they like, or about places they like to go, for example.

This activity also helps children learn about:
expressing the emotion of love.

Quick Tricks for Language ©2001 Monday Morning Books, Inc.

Closet Book
A Quick Trick with Catalogs and Ads

Gather These Materials:
a premade book containing 6 pages, 1 book for each child
markers
scissors
catalogs, junk mail, advertising circulars
glue or glue sticks

Where: at a table

How: With your group of children, talk about closets and what goes in them. Discuss that many closets contain clothing and shoes, but some closets hold sporting goods, hobby supplies, linens, or outdoor items. Talk about what might go in those closets.

Give each child a premade book and have the children use markers to make the book covers look like closet doors. Have the children look in catalogs and other ads for pictures of things that might belong in a closet. Have them cut out those pictures and glue them into their books. Write on their pages the words they dictate about each item. Read the finished books with the children, then let them read to you and to each other.

Variation:
Make a "dresser drawer" book, "car" book, "lunch box" book, "book bag" book, and so on, filled with pictures of appropriate items. Let the children suggest similar books to make.

This activity also helps children learn about:
sorting items that belong together.

Dear Parents,

We are making and reading our own books at school. Your child will be bringing these home from time to time. Let him read them to you. Keep them in a special place to show that you value his growing reading ability.

At first, your child will be "reading" the pictures in his books. Over time, he will begin to focus more attention on the words. Eventually your child will be reading just the words, but looking at the pictures as reminders of what's on the page.

You can help this process by making reading and writing materials available at home. As you see the kinds of books we are making, you might want to make simple books at home, too. The "Quick Trick" below will give you an idea to get you started. You might also want to make up a number of blank books to keep on hand so your child can draw pictures, "write," and read his own stories whenever he desires.

A Quick Trick with Furniture Advertisements

Gather These Materials:
several sheets of plain paper
stapler and staples
construction paper (optional)
advertising or catalogs from furniture stores
scissors
glue or glue stick
markers or crayons
pen

Where: at a table

How: Stack several sheets of paper and staple them along the left side to form a simple book. If desired, add a cover of construction paper.

With your child, look at the furniture advertisements, focusing on the sofas. Talk about sofas and some of the ways a sofa is used. Talk about what you and your family do on the sofa. Give your child the blank book and some advertising circulars. Have him cut out one picture of a sofa to glue to his book cover.

Inside the book, have your child use markers or crayons to draw pictures, one per page, of sofas and of ways a sofa is used. Use a pen to write his dictated words in his book.